Other books by Michael D. Brown
God Created Poetry
A Bridge over the Stars
The Addendum to Perfection
Vanity Prayers
Functional Insanity
Choreographing Words
Infallible Proofs for the Doctrine of Eternal Security

In loving memory of my father, James H. Brown Sr. 2/28/34 to 9/05/2007

Memoirs from my father

On September 5th 2007, my father, age 73 passed from this life into the everlasting arms of God. He left behind a story which he wanted passed down to his family in book form. This work is a true story. It is not concerned with presenting an exhaustive portrait of any one member of the family. To this end I am presenting the story that he shared with me over the past forty nine years. The story is not presented in any particular order. Some of the relatives tell their story to my father by my grandfather or grandmother. The oral tradition so prevalent in African American culture now finds a place in this collection.

The cover of this book is graced by a photo of my father and mother. The picture was taken in the early 1950s before my parents were married. I chose this snapshot for the cover because it is my favorite photograph. It captures something of the grace and eloquence that both my parents presented throughout their lives. They set a very high standard which is rarely seen today. This picture tells a story of a couple living in trying times and of the surpassing grace that they received to overcome adversity. Together they raised and educated six children while working, attending college, maintaining a home and pursuing other personal and professional endeavors.

The most important legacy my parents left is the rich faith that we share in Jesus Christ our Lord. I am comforted with the knowledge of their personal faith and their salvation which is steadfast and unmovable. When the day comes that I close my eyes in this life I will once again open them and see my loved ones who arrived there before me.

For now I can only enjoy my father's memoirs.

My father, James H. Brown Sr. was by all accounts a remarkable man. I am blessed to have had the honor of being raised by a man who loved his family. He was more than just a great provider, he was a real father. While he was very busy working as the first African American, personnel manager for General Electric in the early 1970s in Syracuse, New York, he never missed any important event in my life. I marvel as an adult how he could have accomplished so many things and still raise six children. My father was a man of devotion and great conviction. He was always highly visible and never inaccessible. Everything he did with the family was an opportunity to teach a valuable lesson. I recall the game we played at the dinner table following the meal. Father would point to one of the children and say it's your turn to present.

We never knew who would be called upon to speak. We only knew that it could happen to any of us at any time. He gave us two minutes and a topic we would or should have known something about. After we presented the rest of the family gave a critique and we learned from these exercises.

My father was the consummate teacher always giving instruction and providing inspiration. One of my fondest memories is the time he spent reading the poetry of Emily Dickinson to me. This act cultivated a love for language and reading; ultimately a love for poetry and prose. Few gifts have been so attractive a garland about my neck.

Who can estimate the value of the presence and the love of a wonderful father?

Memoirs from my father

My great grandfather, Joe Christopher Brown is the oldest male in the family that my father spoke of. Joe was born in the late 1800s in Anniston Alabama.
He died in 1926 and was believed to have been relatively young. Joe worked in the foundries like so many other young black males. Joe was a laborer in the commercial pipe shop. I saw for the first time this year a picture of Joe. He was a very light skin black male who could almost pass for white. He most certainly must have come from mixed heritage. His Mother's name is Georgia Brown and her birth date and place are unknown.
Joe had two brothers, Josh and Sam. Sam lived in Gasden, Alabama approximately thirty-one miles north of Anniston. Joe was married to Mamie Coleman Brown who was also of obvious mixed heritage. Mamie; however appears to be a black Native American. Her features are very distinctive; broad nose and high cheek bones. She looks completely Native American except for her skin color which is African or a little darker than medium brown.

Mamie was originally from Talladega, Alabama and she was considered a Creed, Native American Indian. She had two children before she met and married Joe Christopher Brown. A son and a daughter were produced from her first marriage. Mamie was a homemaker caring for her two children. The family reports that Mamie was difficult to get along with and after Joe died she moved from living with one relative to another. Father reports that she moved in with his family when he was very young. He recalls the horse and the open wagon with all of her things pulling up in front of the house. Mamie would stay for maybe six months and then it was time to move on.

Mamie was also given to partiality when it came to her grandchildren. Her favorite was my father's older brother, Roger Floyd Brown Jr. Mamie would promise her grandchildren things but would not come through. But she did give many gifts to her favorite grandchild. Mamie eventually married a third time to a man named, Kale Wilson. Kale was a farmer outside of Anniston, Alabama who grew corn and other vegetables. Kale and Mamie did not produce any

children together. Kale had a brother who my father remembers as "Uncle Brown." His name, Brown Wilson; and he is remembered as one of the favorite uncles father had growing up. Brown Wilson is buried in Central City where most of the family members are also buried.
The first child Mamie and Joe had together was my grandfather Roger Floyd Brown Sr. I grew up knowing my grandfather very well because he was right here living in Syracuse, New York. He was a very strong man with a stately appearance. Roger was a very well spoken, articulate man like my father. He was a Christian pastor who founded, Galilee Baptist Church. He is remembered as a strict disciplinarian and a no-nonsense kind of man. He was direct and let you know just where he was coming from.
He played semi-professional baseball in the Negro league. He was a pitcher for a team called the "Dooley Ditch Anniston Black Rams." The team was part of the National Negro League. The name "Dooley Ditch" came from the fact that a big ditch ran across the outfield. The name, "Anniston Black Rams," was also held by the white baseball team.

Roger was also known for his gospel singing in a group he started called the "Alabama Jubilee singers." The group practiced singing at Roger's home at 1703 ½, McDaniel Ave. The group travelled throughout the south from church to church ministering to the saints.

Earlier this year my father took me to visit this house where he grew up. It is a light slate green home with shingles. These homes were called "shot gun" houses years ago. This home had just three rooms running straight through. It was uncommon for these structures to have a bathroom inside. Absent were the many amenities we enjoy today. Life was very hard back then but that was all that black folks knew. Father tells me that they were very poor but they didn't know that they were.

In many ways it was a much more simple life. They did not own multiple pairs of shoes. It was even common to see young black boys with no shoes on their feet all summer long. Some came to school without shoes or wore the same pair all year long.

Clothing had to last a very long time and it was always washed by hand and hung out to dry. If you owned more than one or two outfits you had more than most people.

During the Great Depression, my grandfather would travel by running and jumping aboard a moving train. This practice which many black men followed was known as, "Ho-Bo-In." When the train stopped at the next town they would go door to door asking for work or food. Times were very tough and people pulled together sharing what little they had, even with total strangers. Finding work was not easy during those days but grandfather was faithful and diligent to look. It was only by the grace of God that he made it.

During a singing engagement in Bynum, Alabama (now Eastaboga) at a small county church, Roger met his future wife, my grandmother, Clara Walker. She subsequently moved with him to Anniston where they raised their children. Clara had been married once before and that marriage ended in divorce. It did however produce children. Clara and her first husband, Henry Roberts had three children named, Albert, Gertrude and Willard. Albert is one of my uncles that I spent time with while growing up. I recall making family trips to Anniston from Syracuse over the summers. We would stay for one or two weeks. We always drove down in our Ford Country Squire. It was roomy and it was a very popular family car back in the late sixties. Uncle Albert owned some land and built a very nice home.

He loved working the land and planted a very nice garden. Albert also loved to sing gospel music and serve the Lord. Albert, like his step-father, Roger Floyd Brown Sr. travelled throughout the south singing in Christian churches. He also played semi-professional baseball in the Negro league. He worked for the Anniston Ordinance Depot. This was a government defense plant. Albert grew up living with his grandmother and his sister. Since he was much older than his half-sisters and brothers he never did live with them.

My father got to know his half-brother as an adult. Albert died in December 2004. He had taken a fall and sustained an injury. This would not have been so serious but he came down with pneumonia and died. I attended the funeral with my father and my younger brother Julius. Too often the only time I see most of my relatives who are spread out living all over the country, is at a funeral. Albert had two sons, Albert Roberts Jr. and Jerry. I saw them last at my father's funeral this past September. Gertrude is Albert's sister, my aunt. She was married just once to William Jackson, who is now deceased. They produced one child, a daughter named, Francis. Willard is the third child born to my grandmother, Clara and her first husband, Henry Roberts. Willard did live with the new combined family. At the age of sixteen he ran away from home and joined the circus. He disappeared for six months before returning home. When Willard returned he had a story to tell. The circus that Willard joined had sold him into slavery. He was forced to work in the fields during the day and at night he was locked up in an animal pen. He somehow escaped but did not turn to the local authorities because they were part of this modern day slave trade. It was still a common practice even as late as the 1940s to capture black men and force them into slavery. Willard died in the late 1970s in Milwaukee, Wisconsin. He married Mary Ham but the marriage produced no children. Roger Floyd Brown Jr. is the first child born to the union of Roger Floyd Brown Sr. and Clara Roberts Brown. My uncle Floyd was born 12/30/32 in Anniston, Alabama. Floyd was a very sociable and popular young man. He was well liked by the women he met. He attended Cobb High School. This was the local colored high school. Floyd was known to have several girlfriends at the same time. He would promise gifts to all of them and then fail to follow through. When things began to unravel and Floyd would have been exposed he sent his girlfriends to his younger brother in the hopes that he would cover for him.

The year was 1950 and the US military began recruiting young blacks in Anniston. They marched on the "Dooley Ditch" field daily. This was done before shipping recruits to fort, DEVENS, in the Massachusetts Army base. The Army recruited young men ages 17 and 18. Floyd served two years in the Army before he rejoined his family which now resided in Syracuse, New York in 1952. In July 1950

Roger got an invitation from his first cousin, Josephine Brown-Herd to come to Syracuse. There Roger hoped to find work and subsequently send for the family. He did find work at Frazier and Jones foundry. He sent money to the family in Anniston as often as he could.

The family in Alabama survived in Roger's absence with the whole family pulling together. The next son to Roger and Clara is James Houston Brown, Sr. (my father). James was named after a catcher on the baseball team which Roger pitched for. James lived with his parents and siblings in Anniston until he was sixteen years old. He recounts working in a restaurant that same summer. The restaurant was called the "Noble Inn." James washed dishes and helped the cooks with food preparation. This type of work was common for black males. He worked that summer to help support the family as they made plans to migrate north. One night the restaurant was short staffed and they asked James to wait on tables. The patrons laughed, jeered and mocked James. The whites were amused and upset to see, a black male publically serving white patrons in this capacity. Growing up in Anniston in the thirties and forties was very different for people of color than their white counterparts. Under total segregation there was no mixing of whites and coloreds. Signs were prominently displayed forbidding violations with the understanding that coloreds would face severe consequences.

Social life for blacks in Anniston was better than up north. For example there were black owned theaters. In Anniston on 15th street there was Jim's theater. Here films like, "Cabin in the sky"; "The blood of Jesus", and even black westerns entertained and educated us. Historically black colleges reached out to make college affordable for black students. More blacks graduated from high school under segregation than those blacks living in the northern cities like Syracuse, NY. There were black businesses like grocery stores, barber shops, shoe repair, and dentist, like Dr. Rogers and Son in Anniston. Blacks that had their own businesses fared better than those struggling to find work from whites. At that time there were no pensions for coloreds who reached retirement age. There was of course Social Security, which Kale called, "Getting my pennies." The church played an important role in many ways. The Browns worshipped God on Sundays attending, Friendship Baptist Church. Rev. White, a light skin, colored man with gold teeth was the pastor of the flock. Sunday school began at 9:30am, ending an hour later. Sunday morning service began at 11:00 am. One noticeable difference between that church and the churches of today is their involvement with the boy scouts. Boys at church were heavily mentored in the scouts. They went on camping trips and were taught many things. Men spent time teaching young boys how to be men and carry themselves with dignity. They learned how to fish and values were instilled in them. Women and young girls stayed home for the most part. They were not deeply involved out in the public arena. When young women reached sixteen they were presented to society with a debutant ball. The men in the family were escorts for their daughters and sisters. In Anniston it was Cobb High School, where so many young black females had their ball. There was also social life in the kiddies club every Saturday morning at 9:00am at the Ritz Theater. Here for five bread wrappers from Lloyd's bakery one gained admission. James got in for free by collecting used wrappers customers discarded from Jeff's barbecue stand. (Black owned)

The movie that was shown at the Ritz was a series not unlike the soap operas of today. There was always a cliff hanger at the end that left you in suspense. This was one of many things that drew patrons back the next week. There were also weekly drawings and gifts were dispensed. The regular movie cost eleven cents for children under twelve and twenty five cents for those older than twelve.

Twice a week the 15th street Catholic Church provided a dance for colored teens. This was an exciting event that drew large crowds. They played black records and young teenagers danced and socialized. James walked to the dance like so many other youngsters. Even before the bus boycott which came some years later, many blacks refused to ride the buses. There were small personal protests to retain a sense of dignity in the face of a very evil system.

Once a week, the Carver Community Center, played a movie outside in the warm night air. It was free for everyone and between one hundred and one hundred fifty people would come. September 1950, came and it was time to make the big move to Syracuse, New York. There was no moving truck filled with furniture, clothing and a lifetime of belongings. There were only two large cardboard boxes. The trip was kept secret from almost everyone. Roger sent what he thought would be enough to cover the bus fare for his wife and four children that were still living with them. Floyd Jr., was in the Army by this time. James, Evelyn, Clara Mae, and Wallace were the four minors still living at home.

Grandma Clara called for a taxi and made her way with her four children to the Greyhound bus station. She had the children wait in the colored only section while she attempted to purchase the tickets. To her surprise she was five dollars short. Immediately she sent James two or three blocks away to a family friend to borrow the money.

Sweetie Curry was the family friend who came to the rescue. She knew the family well and didn't ask any questions. Sweetie, known as Aunt Sweetie, had years earlier rented a place to Roger and Clara. James took the money from Sweetie who was working at the Jefferson Hotel and hurried back to catch the Greyhound bus. Five dollars was a lot of money to a large family living on very little in those difficult times. How would Clara feed four children for two days on a long trip? She had no money and even if she did the restaurants the bus would stop at would not serve colored people. Clara planned ahead packing chicken sandwiches in a shoe box. The family boarded the Greyhound bus at 6:00pm on Friday arriving in Syracuse, New York on Sunday at 11:00 am. Wallace was the youngest child born to Roger and Clara. His 9th birthday arrived during the two day trip. After the bus passed the Mason Dickson line the colored passengers could sit anywhere they pleased on the bus. The family met a very nice white gentleman who gave Wallace fifty cents for his birthday. This was a very kind thing to do and really a wonderful gift considering its value during the fifties. Evelyn the oldest daughter born to Roger and Clara had spent the last school year in Syracuse at Matson, Junior High school. She was now returning to Syracuse with her family after spending her last summer in Anniston. She had lived her first year in Syracuse with Josephine, her father's cousin. Making such a move involved the whole family pulling together with many sacrifices. Clara took in washing as did many colored women. She washed white peoples' clothes by hand on a wash board. These boards were called scrub boards.

The clothes were hung out to dry and then ironed by using the old fashioned irons without electricity. The irons were placed on hot coals and when one cooled off it was replaced by a second. The clothes were neatly folded and ready for pick up. Roger loved to look nice when he hung out at Dr. Roger's drug store where his friends gathered. He would borrow the nice clothing of the white men and return it unbeknown to them. His friends thought he had a lot of money to always dress so well. Roger however, had little to no money. He worked in the pipe shop with many other colored men who did foundry work. Clara worked hard as well during the Great Depression. She cooked meals for a white family three times a day. She would make sandwiches from the extra food and wrap it for Roger who would pick up the food left outside on top of a garbage can. She made $2.25 per week until another colored woman offered to do her job for $2.00 per week. She had to accept less money to keep her job. I never met my grandmother Clara since she died about one week before I was born. She lived here in Syracuse about eight years before her death. She worked for Syracuse University Chancellor, William Tolley as his housekeeper.

Colored men had a very difficult time finding work during the depression and many went to C.C. camps living in Government dorms to perform piecemeal work. This involved cleaning streets, highways and parks.

When the family arrived in Syracuse in September 1950, it was at the Greyhound bus station located on Harrison St. They walked from there to 710 Almond St to live with Josephine. The house was a four family owned by Josephine in a predominantly Jewish section of Syracuse.

The family was supposed to have an apartment in the house; but because a tenant had not yet moved out, the Browns were forced to set up their new residence in the basement. This went on for nine months. The first day following their arrival to Syracuse was Monday and it was a school day.

James first day was one he would never forget. At lunch time he made the mistake of sitting at a table with two white male students. One of them said to him, “I don’t want a Nigger, sitting in front of me.” There were only about twenty students of color attending Syracuse Central High school. (Now Central Tech)

James was just sixteen years old entering school as a junior and felt completely alone. It is hard to imagine what it must have felt like. Another colored student named, Ulysses Adam came up to James and told him to come and sit at the colored table with several other black male students. Their names are Emmanuel Breland, Richard Breland, Clarence Dunham (Junie Dunham), and Leroy Jackson. These students of color stuck together and are still close friends some fifty years later.

James determined to make a name for himself through baseball. There was only one other colored student playing baseball on the school team. James would be the second that week of try outs in May 1951. James normally played catcher but there was an opening as second basemen. The chances of making the team were much better if he tried out for second base. He made the decision and was successful.

James was not used to playing second base and not long into the season sustained an injury when he was struck in the mouth with the baseball.

James would lose his two front teeth due to this injury. He was further embarrassed when the coach had to bring him home and saw where he was living. It took many months before he could have his teeth properly repaired and this was an especially difficult time for him. James became somewhat shy and kept to himself as he did not want anyone to notice how poorly his teeth looked. Clara was not happy to discover James had an accident playing baseball. She did not say much to the coach as she was not comfortable speaking in difficult situations.

Clara was not formally educated having only finished the sixth grade. Roger had only completed the 11th but was a very good speaker and handled himself with finesse.

While social life was better for colored families in the segregated south there weren't many opportunities for work for black males. Up north Roger owned his first car, a 1948 Buick. His second car was a canary yellow 1955 Ford. This was quite an accomplishment for a man of modest means and very humble beginnings. Roger drove this car back home to Anniston to show all of his family and friends. Trips back to Anniston were common and I have been introduced to all of my first cousins and some I have gotten to know well as I was growing up.

Military service came immediately after graduating from high school. James joined the US Air Force, 10/17/52. James went to basic training at Samson Air Force base, in Geneva NY and recalls that basic was extended from six weeks to thirteen because of an incident where American soldiers were killed by a surprise attack while they were asleep in their tents. James did well in training and his tactile instructor Sergeant, Kettles appointed him to handle the scheduling of guard duty for the troops. One white soldier commented to James, “I noticed that you are fair with the scheduling.” “My father told me that if blacks get in positions of authority they will use it against whites like whites have done to blacks.” Another incident James recalls is befriending a white French soldier who was a part of the same unit. They were traveling on a train which broke down. A bus picked them up and the soldiers went to a hotel in town. That evening they were able to eat at the Greyhound station which had a restaurant inside. However in the morning that same restaurant refused to serve the colored soldiers. Three other restaurants also refused to serve them. The Frenchman was amazed to see how poorly colored American soldiers were treated. He commented that he was not an American and could get service and yet American born colored soldiers could not.

During his military service James became ill and was hospitalized and treated with a new and popular drug. This new drug (Penicillin), however, made James condition worse. He was actually allergic and the doctors did not figure this out. James became so ill that he almost died. He was moved to another facility and his weight dropped dramatically. James over heard one doctor say to another that he did not expect him to live throughout the night.

It was then that James began to pray to the Lord and asked God to deliver him from death. James recalls that God did answer his prayer and directed him to stop taking the medicine that the doctors were giving him. He sensed God's presence in his room and said, "It was like a shadow was passing in and moving around the room." James obeyed the instructions and rapidly improved. He later admitted to the doctors that he stopped taking the drugs. The doctors told him that they thought he could tolerate the drugs well because of his complexion. They thought at that time that fair skin people were the ones who might have a problem with this drug. James was subsequently released from military duty due to his illness with an honorable discharge.

James returned to Syracuse immediately and secured work with a washing machine manufacturer named, Easy Washer. James worked here as a laborer and made $1.35 per hour. He kept this job for 3 years (1953-1956). There were times when the company would lay off workers and then call them back to work when their production needs called for it. James got an offer to work for General Electric which ended up being a very good move. He looked back and marveled at how God's blessing carried him for 34 years and even included a wonderful pension and retirement.

General Electric proved to be a crucible of testing for him. It was the late 1950s and early 1960s. General Electric had not hired many people of color or placed them in non-traditional roles. James began for just his first month as an accumulator in the stock room; which means he pulled parts needed on the assembly line. Next he became a stock keeper, which was a promotion to supervisor over the accumulators. Some other employees complained about his rapid promotion; but the manager told James that he was promoted because he knew more about his job after just one month than the others knew in three months. Next he was again promoted in just a few months to a non-exempt salaried position. He was now a production clerk. This lasted just six months before he was laid off. He was told that when business picked up he would return to a salaried job. He was called back and the union sent him to the stock room again. He was not there long before he was recalled to the stock room with a salaried job as a dispatcher.

James recounts that his first real trouble came when he was a production clerk. There was a great deal of discrimination which reflects the times and James felt the brunt of it. His immediate supervisor was extremely prejudiced and he made life at work for James miserable. James considered quitting but he had a wife and family by this time and had them to consider. Another manager approached James and explained to him that he must not quit. The company purposefully placed him there to expose certain things that they believed were happening. It was just a week later than James was moved to a better job. It was now the 1960s and James was very involved in community activities. A manager at work recommended him for a position in personnel.

He was interviewed five times over a period of time and finally offered the job. During this process Dr. Martin Luther King Jr., was shot to death and there was great upheaval throughout the country as a result. General Electric was facing a large fine by the Federal Government for past acts of discrimination. Women and minorities could not hold certain jobs. James was told he had the skills necessary to be a line foreman but they were afraid that the whites would not work for him. This kept James from certain higher level promotions. The job in personnel was to be a precursor of what would subsequently become the manager of equal opportunity.

Part of James duties required him to identify managers who were prone to discriminate. James also was a placement specialist in personnel in charge of interviewing and hiring. He subsequently spear headed the "Yes" program. This special project recruited young high school students for summer jobs. These students in many cases were the least likely to find success because of their family history and background. James refused to use color and poverty as predictors for success and hired students that other companies would not consider. The first group of students began in 1968. Approximately 200 students viewed as under -privileged from the inner city.

This summer was also a time of personal loss as Wallace Brown, James uncle and Roger Brown's brother died of lung cancer. Wallace was a heavy smoker and had been for many years.

During work James would question the white workers in the factory. He wanted to know how they felt about working side by side with the inner city students who were coming for summer jobs. He inquired about their attitudes and mainly wanted to know if the students of color would be received.

Many of the whites made negative comments and felt that the colored students did not want to work nor would they perform their job duties. Once the students James hired began working they proved the concerns of the whites to be completely unwarranted.

While James was extremely busy and even perhaps over extended he enrolled in Syracuse University to work towards his bachelor's degree. This was a heavy load considering his job, marriage and growing family.

James met and married Thelma Jean Curry after just four months of courting her. They met on James 20th birthday at Bethany Baptist Church. Located at that time on Harrison St. James arrived late to the weekly youth gathering of the church on Sunday evening. He and his father, Roger had driven to Rome, NY earlier that day getting lost while learning the route. The trip to Rome is relatively short but some wrong turns cost them additional time. When they arrived at church, James was surprised with an unexpected birthday celebration. He was also introduced to his future wife.

He escorted Thelma home that evening after church and that was the beginning of my immediate family.

There are six children altogether. Joanne, James Jr., Michael, Bobby, Janet, and Julius. We were fortunate to move into our first home in the 1960s.

It was located on Meredith Ave in Nedrow, NY. I recall the house as a barn shaped structure. It had an open porch in the front of the house and steps in the rear. There was land surrounding on all sides of the house. The land was barren and very dry when we first moved in. A very tall tree stood almost forbidding us to the right side of the house. Both sides in front of the house had ditches that filled up when it rained hard. Often times the sewers would back up.

I recall the day several trucks pulled up and dumped dirt in our yard. We jumped up and down for joy thinking how much fun we were going to have playing in all that dirt. Of course father had other plans for that dirt. We spent the next few years fixing the dry brittle cracked ground with this new dirt. When we finished the grounds looked amazing. What a transformation. The driveway to the house was very long and we constantly swept it. In the winter we went out to shovel and it could take a few hours to clean this lengthy driveway.

The house had three bedrooms. Mother and father had the master bedroom which was at the top of the stairs and around the corner at the end of the hall. The only bathroom was just to the immediate right at the top of the stairs; next came the boys' bedroom just to the right of the bathroom and the girls' room to the right of the boys' room. Since there were four boys we all slept in bunk beds. The girls had more room and a little nicer arrangement.

We had it pretty good compared to my father's home that he grew up in. That house was a three room shot-gun style home. You could walk straight through it in less than a half minute. Everybody slept together in one room and even one bed.

Very little privacy, space or comfort for them at that time. They did have running water but it was only cold water. They used lamps since they had no electricity. It seems so hard to imagine that life was so primitive, even third world, just a generation ago.

Father was a strict disciplinarian and mother tried to follow suit but she was a very gentle and tender hearted lady who spoke softly. Mother was not the contentious type and would not argue nor joust with six children. Father on the other hand seemed to have endless energy. He worked two jobs and went to college and always did a lot of work around the house with his sons. He made time to take us boys to the park and play catch with a baseball. He purchased a glove for each of us and taught us how to use it. He nurtured in us a love for sports.

He also was big on reading and writing and I especially enjoyed hearing him read poetry. There were always plenty of books in the house. Magazines also came in the mail and we loved reading JET and EBONY. Father never allowed us to use slang or foul language. We were expected to speak well and mastering the English language was a daily task. Father was not afraid to correct us if we did not use good diction or enunciate our words properly.

Father use to ask the question, "Where will you be in five years?" I grew up thinking about this and it is still a question I ask myself today. It caused me to plan and to consider tomorrow and to redeem time. It is after all our most precious commodity. Each of my siblings is very different as maybe expected as we are all individuals. People sometimes think that because you have the same parents and you were raised the same way, that you all come out basically the same. This is not true at all and my siblings are a testimony to that fact. Joanne is the oldest and she is very stubborn and head strong. From the beginning she has always been determined to do things her own way and never did care much about consequences. She also developed a visceral attitude towards authority. This trait is also present in my older brother James (Jimmy) who has become a wanderer, who rarely contacts other members of the family. Jimmy is a very gifted artist who has tremendous potential which has gone unrecognized. I am the third child born to James and Thelma. I cannot objectively critique my own life. Bobby is next and he is much like mother a very tender hearted lovable soul. Janet passed away at the tender age of twenty six, on the 4th of July. She accepted Christ just weeks before she died and she is sorely missed.

Janet never married nor had any children. She did graduate from college completing an Associates degree.

Lastly there is Julius who seems to have all of the gifts and talents from his siblings combined. Julius, is multi-talented and multi-faceted.

He is hard to sum up not because he is difficult to understand but because this book has length limitations. I am especially proud of Julius, as was father because Julius recently graduated from college and is now a practicing Registered Nurse. He graduated in the top of his class and has made this family very proud. Julius did very well graduating with honors from high school years ago. He went directly into the Marine Corp instead of college. I was the first of my siblings to go to and graduate from college with a four year degree and now a Masters. Julius however has accomplished something special because he returned to school later in life. How much more difficult it is when you have a wife and four children to care for?

Each of my siblings has been blessed with some special gift or talent. We all do not work to our full potential and this is something I wish to see realized in my own life. I remember my sister Janet was the one sibling that wrote faithfully to me when I was in college. Those were lonely days for me being so far from home. I would wait with the other college students by the mail box hoping for some word from home and when I got a letter from Janet, I was elated. Janet called me from Los Angeles where she was living before she died. We had a great conversation about the Lord and how she had just accepted him and looked forward to her new life in Christ. It was a day or two later that she was taken from this life. A day does not go by without her inhabiting my thought life. I recall a fishing trip we went on with father. Normally he just took the boys but Janet cried saying she wanted to go too. Well her tears prcvailed and she caught more fish than all of us put together. One summer day, Father asked me to come home from college and spend the summer with Janet. She was living on Fayette St. In her own apartment and she was still very young. Father wanted her to be safe and also supervised. I had a hard time keeping up with her fast paced life but I did keep the young men who tried to talk to her away. Janet was a very attractive woman with a yellowish complexion and her hair turned a ruddy brownish red in the summer. She had a personality that drew people to her and she was very loyal to family and friends. Janet's best friend Tyan Crowder, married our older brother James becoming his 2nd wife. The marriage was very short and ended within six months. James has two sons from his first marriage, James III, Steven and a step son named Alan. James married a third time to a flight attendant named, Anna from Mexico but that marriage also ending quickly.

Joanne has been married just once and has yet to divorce her estranged husband, Alfred Danzy of more than twenty years. They have one son together, Alfred Danzy Jr. He is nicknamed, Alfie and now married to Tweety and they have two children.

Bobby was married and is now divorced and his marriage to Sonja did not produce any children.

Julius is married with three sons: Bernardo, Bryant, Jermel and one daughter Ashley. Julius wife's name is Raquel. They have been married for over twenty years. This is Julius second marriage. The first produced no children and lasted just a few weeks.

I am also on my second marriage the first ending after 19 years in divorce. The 1st marriage produced two daughters: Shekinah Marie Brown, and Hannah Bethel Brown. Neither of my daughters is married nor have children at this time. The most recent addition to the family is a baby girl which my niece had this summer. The baby is called Alana Janet Marie. I am now married as of May 3rd 2006 to Stephanie Ann Hicks. We are raising Rafael her son from her first marriage.

Thus far I have mentioned seven generations of this family from the direct line of Georgia Brown, Joe Christopher and Roger Brown, Sr.

I would be remiss if I did not recount a very sad time for this family which occurred a week before my birth. It was the summer of 1958, the end of June. The family had been in Syracuse for seven years. There was a family reunion planned and a trip to Syracuse from Alabama was organized. It was Clara's side of the family and this was their first trip to Syracuse. They came in two cars and Clara was busy cleaning and shopping, preparing for the arrival of the family. Her brothers and sisters with their spouses were all coming for the happy reunion. They left Anniston on a Friday afternoon to arrive in Syracuse late Saturday. Jimmy met Clara Friday at 4pm on East Adams Street at Loblaws, grocery store. Clara was gathering up a lot of food for the reunion. She was very excited about the prospect of seeing her brothers and sisters and their spouses. Jimmy helped Clara with the groceries and then hurried home because his wife, Thelma was due to have the baby at any moment. It was 10pm and the phone rang. It was Roger Floyd Brown Sr. calling his son James to tell him to rush over. Clara was unable to stop vomiting and was in great pain. At first they attempted to take her in the car but she was in too much pain. An ambulance had to be called. She was rushed to Crouse Irving hospital. They waited there at the hospital for close to two hours and Clara was admitted. James returned home and the hospital proceeded to do some tests.

The next morning Jimmy and Clara sat bedside talking about the reunion. Clara was anxious to return home knowing she had company coming. She wanted to be home in time to greet her family. She told her son Jimmy to go home, "You have a baby coming." "Don't leave Thelma there alone."

"That girls gonna have that baby." Less than an hour later a knock on the door at Jimmy's apartment over on Harrison St. Roger was there standing with tears streaming down his face. This was the first time Jimmy ever saw his father cry. Roger said that Clara (Jimmy's mother) was dead.

While they stood in the hospital in shock, the doctor wanted to perform an autopsy but Roger refused. He kept saying, "No, No" Jimmy finally convinced his father, Roger to allow it. Whatever caused her death might be something in the family. The autopsy results revealed that an artery leading to the heart had burst. This may have been due to the excitement or some other factors. Clara was just 49 when she passed away. I am 49 and I can now appreciate just how young she was when she died.

Roger instructed his son Jimmy and his other children to bring the family which was arriving from Anniston to the house. He told them do not tell them about Clara's passing until they are home and no longer in the street or traveling. They met the two car loads and of course everyone was glad to be off the road after driving close to twenty hours. A few moments passed before one of Clara's sisters asked, "Where is she?" Suddenly a hush fell over the room. Roger spoke and said, "She passed away this morning."

A call was placed to Anniston and now two cars filled with more family were coming for another reason.

A funeral had to be arranged quickly, especially with so many family members present. What was to be a joyous occasion was now an awful tragedy. The funeral took place July 1st, 1958. It was sorrow enduring for more than just a night. The next day I was born at what I imagine must have been a most inopportune time. I am filled with sorrow to this day because I never met Grandmother Clara and I only have stories about her. I hear pain and sorrow upon sorrow in my father's voice when he speaks of losing her. I only recently understand that sorrow and pain with the loss of my own dear father.

Whenever Father introduced me to relatives he would preference it by telling them that I was the one who came the day after mother was buried.

I have the distinction of being born out of the due time. I was however blessed to have a grandmother on my mother's side. Her name is Gladys Briscoe. She was very special to me and always made me feel that I was deeply loved. She made me feel like Joseph with his coat of many colors. When my birthday came she would always give me more money than my sisters and brothers. I resembled my own mother, her only child and this endeared me to her. I was crushed when she died in the mid eighties. She was really like a mother to me. So many members of my family have died young.

I also never got to know my uncle Mark Irons who married my aunt Clara Mae, who was named after Grandmother Clara. Mark died at the age of 26. Mark and Clara were separated for a short time before Clara's first child (El Rico) was born. Clara spent part of her pregnancy living with her brother Jimmy and his wife, Thelma. She was reunited with her husband for the balance of the pregnancy. Clara had to have surgery and was bedridden. Mark got up, went to the kitchen to get her some milk and passed out. Clara called Jimmy saying, “Mark passed out I think he’s dead.” It was later determined that he died of walking pneumonia. Jimmy only had one car and it was at the hospital with Thelma who used it to get to work. It was 12:30 or 1:00am by then Mark was pronounced dead. His life seemly, cut short. Mark was part of a singing group in Syracuse which produced a record that is occasionally still played on the radio. The song is called, “Don’t put all your eggs in one basket.” The group was called, “Otis and the all night workers.” Clara Mae obtained some serious scarring on her lungs as a pre-teenager in the south due to her contracting pneumonia. She had trouble as an adult and this was complicated because she was a smoker. She had one lung removed and was advised not to smoke any more. After her release from the hospital she was also advised not to go up and down the stairs. This was difficult because her home was a two story with stairs. This restriction was to last for at least one month giving her body time to heal. Clara unfortunately resumed smoking and she was also too active for her weaken state of health. Her older brother Floyd was planning a barbeque and Clara was busy handing out flyers to everyone. Jimmy received a call that Clara had passed out. She was taken to Memorial hospital not far from where she lived. Jimmy recalls that he arrived to find her on life support. This was due to her heart not beating on its own. Jimmy went home and called his siblings apprising them of the situation. He returned to the hospital staying until midnight and returned home once more. Before reporting to work the next day Jimmy called to check on his sister and he was advised that she had passed away. Clara Mae died on her 46th birthday. An autopsy proved that she died from walking pneumonia.

I was a young adult when she passed and I have wonderful memories of Aunt Clara, who we called "Aunt Nook." She was a spontaneous, fun-loving person. She loved music and attended lots of shows and concerts. I remember one Jazz and R&B festival she attended with her brother Jimmy in Cleveland, Ohio. Clara had three children: El-Rico, LaRonda, and Corey. Rico died young and I recall performing the eulogy. His sister LaRonda or Ronnie as she is fondly called is cherished by the whole family. Every time she walks into a room she is swamped by any family member that is present. LaRonda, is a deeply spiritual highly inspirational woman of God. She is a motivator and just a great joy to be around. She has a son named Wilson and they reside currently in Chicago. Corey is Clara Mae's youngest and he resides in Syracuse with his wife "Niece" and his son and daughter.

It was just three months ago that I sat on the porch with my father eating a slice of watermelon. It was a hot day in August 2007. He was concerned that we hurry and finish this book. I deeply regret that it was not finished in time for him to see the end product. There were unexpected problems with my laptop and also waiting for pictures from relatives.

That hot day in August Dad said Michael we must also record my mother's side of the family.

Up until then we had only covered things from grandfather's side. So then beginning with grandmother, Clara Walker Brown we must record the other half of father's family.
Clara Walker Brown was born the daughter of Elbert Walker and Ella Miller Walker. Elbert is the son of Samuel Walker and Amanda Patterson Walker. Elbert was blind and is remembered as a tobacco chewer who would sit on the porch of the relative he happened to be staying with and spit tobacco onto the ground. The children had to be careful as they played in front of the house so as not to be in his line of fire. James H. Brown Sr. remembers his grandfather on his mother's side briefly. "He would come and stay for a short time maybe a few months and then stay with another relative." He is remembered living with James and family in the second home they lived in which was on the same street as the first. Both houses were the same style home and both were relatively small. Samuel Walker appears to be a white man or perhaps of immediate mixed heritage. Along with Elbert he had two other sons who were twins: Oscar and Arthur.

Oscar lived to be 103 years old and spent his life in Central City. Arthur died young. James remembers that Arthur was laid out in his death on a cooling board. This was a custom of that time in our communities.

When someone died in the poor black community the body was kept at home and placed on a cooling board, sometimes an ironing board was used. This took place for about two days giving family and friends time to view the body and also to have a pine box built to place the body in.

Men from the family and sometimes neighbors took a pick axe and shovel to dig the grave. It wasn't always deep enough and animals sometimes would dig up remains. The smell of bodies in the grave yards was another problem when they were not secured properly. James remembers when Arthur died and his body was placed on such a cooling board. Outside during the viewing there were bed sheets hanging on the line. James and other small children were scared by the sight of the white sheets; they thought Arthur was a ghost who had returned from the dead. Elbert had seven children and fifteen grandchildren. Their names are as follows:

1) Waymond Walker, never had any children.
2) Louise Walker Miller married John Miller (their children): Lenard Miller, Hazel Miller, Catherine Miller, and Joseph Miller.
3) Clara /Albert: Willard, Roger Floyd, Jr. James H. Brown Sr. Evelyn, Clara Mae, and Wallace Jr.
4) Walker Garrett married to Carl Garrett: daughters, Dorothy and Mary Jo.
5) Hercules Levon Walker married Louise Holloway: Son-Hercules Jr. Daughters; Deborah & Stella.
6) Marguerite died young never having any children.
7) Laris Walker married Martha Dean Story: Elbert, James, Jewel, Jerald, Maxine and Diane.

   Hercules Jr. is reported to have been a gangster and died a violent death being shot while driving his car out of town. The murderer was quickly apprehended as the murder was seen by witnesses and the police caught the culprit immediately as he was attempting to drag the body from one car to another.

During the mid thirties there were white merchants or peddlers as they were called on the streets in the black communities. They would sell fruits and vegetables from the horse drawn wagons. The Negro women were referred to by these merchants by a slang term pronounced, "Ain'tee." This was slang for aunt and it was used as a derogatory term. My grandfather Roger tells how Clara responded to this one day when a white peddler called her by this term. Clara threw her arms around the peddler and said, "I know we have some whites in the family and you are the proof." I can only imagine what the white peddler's reaction must have been to be hugged and kissed by a colored woman in public.

From the many stories my father has shared with me about Clara Walker Brown, I can sense she was a courageous woman -she must have been. She must have been tempered with a great sense of humor and a toughness to survive so many hardships.

Hearing about her life helps to explain things I see in my own life and in that of my siblings. Clara and Roger produced another daughter my aunt, Evelyn born on March 3rd, 1936 in Anniston Alabama. She is a gifted woman who can sing, cook and is an accomplished interior designer. She graduated from Central High School in Syracuse in 1953. She met her first husband Donald Jackson in the mid 1950s at Dunbar Center in Syracuse. They were married after a brief courtship and traveled extensively since Donald was in the US Air Force. Their children are Edward Anthony (Tony) born 1/23/1954. Tony was the first black student body president at McConquah, High School in Bunker Hill, Indiana. He served in 1971-1972. Tony was actively involved in track. Cherly (called Sherry) Andrea Jackson-Karr born 6/8/1955 was involved in cheerleading throughout high school and also cheered three years in college at I.U. Bloomington Indiana. She is married to Mark Karr and has one son named, Jeridan Blair Jackson (12-16-84) from her first marriage. Evelyn's youngest daughter is Clarissa who was born in China in 1958. Her nick name is

“Beaver” and she recently married, Denny Smith and has no children produced from the marriage. Beaver works for General Electric as a human resource executive and travels extensively throughout Europe and Asia. Next is Dwayne Reynard Jackson, who is nick named, “Rinny.” He was born 12/5/59 and is married to Elizabeth Jackson and father to Reid Colin, McKenna, Delaney Nicole and Baylie Jade.

I should also mention Roger Floyd Brown Sr.’s sisters’ children as they are my father’s first cousins and my second. Roger’s sisters are Inez Brown Elston and Edna Mae Brown-Jenkins. Inez has ten children; Clarence Elston Jr. (Bear), Roosevelt (Dee-Dee), Mary Lousie, Eddie Mae, Odessa, Lena, Levon, Ruby, Joanne, and Paul. Edna Mae Brown-Jenkins was married to Leamond Sr. (nicknamed Jabo) Jabo from one of the Jamacian Islands; a dark skin, red eyed man. They had six children together: Queen Esther, Reanell, Leamond Jr., Helen, Willie, and Lula. Roger’s brother Wallace also had a child named Wanda.

My father’s youngest brother, Wallace Levon Brown Jr. and Demetria. All of my father’s siblings have been mentioned and their children. There are a few exceptions; Roger Floyd Brown Jr. has three children: Kirk, Kay and Nikki. I do not know much of their story because I cannot locate them. I may not have their correct formal names. These are the nicknames that we used of them when we were all children. Lastly there is Rosetta who is my aunt and half sister of my father. She entered our lives after we were adults. I met her for the first time in the mid 1980s.

During the writing of this book my father James H. Brown Sr. died. He was determined to have a record of the family history produced. Several deaths occurred as we continued to move forward towards completion. I am pleased that God gave me some very special time over the past two years with my father. We traveled south to Anniston twice in recent years and viewed the home father grew up in. I saw the community center where he played baseball and enjoyed movies on hot summer nights.

We walked through streets where he rode his bicycle and drove past many sites that brought wonderful memories to mind for my father.

On September 5th, 2007 my father died while he was supervising my nephews and two friends that were helping me to move my belonging into my father's garage. My wife and I were planning to move into a home next door to my father's property. It was important to father that I record and pass on his memoirs. His death came as quite a surprise and it hit the family very hard. I know that my father would not want me to grieve his death forever. He would not want me to have sorrow upon sorrow. I rejoice to know that he is saved by the grace of God. He is a man of faith and put all of his hope and trust in the Lord Jesus Christ. I am fully persuaded that the day is coming when I will be reunited with my father and all of those who have faith in the blessed Savior and only wise God, Jesus Christ. When I look back at the things that my father enjoyed I am reminded of him in those things. For example a great concert with some old school singers. It was summer 2006 and my father accompanied my wife and me to a jazz festival featuring Smokey Robinson. My dad loved this show and I marveled at Smokey and that incredible evening concert. My mind wants to hold onto every great memory and make it return in my thoughts to stay.

The year was 2005 and we took a trip to Atlantic City with my father. My two daughters and I loved travelling with father. He loved to show us things and he was our family tour guide. Father loved to gamble and he would go at any time. I would not call it an addiction as he was a very occasional gambler. He seemed to win quite a bit and luck was not as good off the table as it was on. In retirement gambling was a recreation for James H. Brown Sr., and that combined with my own love for play gave us something current and in common.

Father made the trip to Las Vegas when Stephanie and I ran off to get married. It was just the three of us and Dad put my new wife and I to shame when we consider the amazing energy he had to walk for hours. He would stay up late gambling mostly at night. During the day he played tour guide and showed us all over the Las Vegas strip. Dad was so kind to even pay for most of the trip as one more wedding gift. I was thrilled that he stood up for me as my best man. He also gave the bride away. This was very special to Stephanie since her own father passed away several years ago.

I'm thankful for all of these memories that were special to him and to all of us as well. I recall that last trip to Anniston Alabama with dad. We went to celebrate the 80th birthday of aunt, Ruth who was married to my father's older half-brother, Albert.

The first trip to Anniston in recent years was to bury uncle, Albert. The second trip was to celebrate Aunt, Ruth's birthday. It was of course a surprise birthday party. It was held in a beautiful hall designed for such special occasions. Aunt, Evelyn handled the decorations and the food and it was exquisite. We enjoyed the family and my daughter Shekinah, got to meet many family members she had never seen before.

Father stopped at the graveyard where many of our people are buried. He spoke of the Miller family and its connection to the Walker family. Finally he showed the tie-in with the Brown family. I notice the names all tied together in certain individuals. I am writing this book for a second reason which I discover as I complete this task. It is to hold on to these wonderful stories. When I am a little older and my memory fades faster that it already is; I can pick up this book and remember the kind, honorable champion of a man that my father strove to become. I will be able to recall in more specific details a time to laugh and a time to rejoice. I will be able to see more clearly that God has made all things beautiful in His own time.

Joe Christopher Brown

Mammie Coleman - Brown

Roger Floyd Brown Sr.
Made 1934

Rev Roger Floyd Brown Sr.
Clara Walker Brown

Roger Floyd Brown Sr.

Rev. Roger Floyd Brown Sr.

Clara Walker Brown

Clara Walker Roberts - Brown

Wallace Brown
The First

James Houston Brown Sr.
Syracuse Central High
June 20, 1952

Left to Right
James H. Brown
Roger F. Brown Jr.

www.ingramcontent.com/pod-product-compliance
Ingram Content Group UK Ltd.
Pitfield, Milton Keynes, MK11 3LW, UK
UKHW041919190726
13854UKWH00003B/1330

9 780615 174105